By Dr. Ref, PhD
Scitenberg Kids

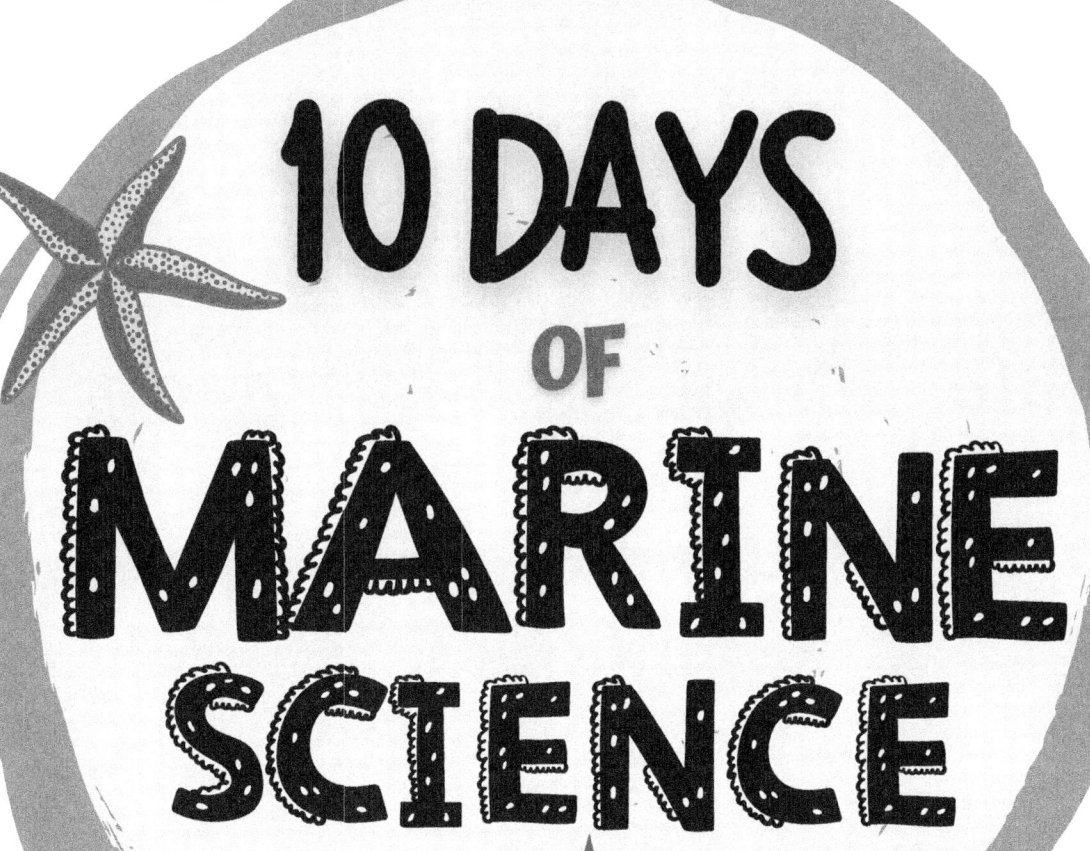

10 DAYS OF MARINE SCIENCE

SHARKS, CURRENTS, CORALS AND MORE!

No part of this book may be reproduced, transmitted, or introduced into a retrieval system in any form or by any means, graphic, electronic, or mechanical, including photocopying, taping and recording, without prior written permission from the author.
Copyright © 2022 Scitenberg
All rights reserved
For more info contact
scitenberg@gmail.com
Follow us on
@scitenberg_
@Scitenberg

10 Days of Marine Science

Day 1 Marine Science ------------- 4

Day 2 The Ocean -- ----------- 8

Day 3 Waves ----------------- 12

Day 4 Tides ------------------ 16

Day 5 Currents ---------------- 20

Day 6 Ocean Life ------------- 24

Day 7 Jellyfish --------------- 28

Day 8 Sharks ---------------- 32

Day 9 Aquaculture ----------- 36

Day 10 Ocean Pollution --------- 40

DAY 1
MARINE SCIENCE

What is marine science?

Marine science also know as Oceanography and Oceanology is the branch of Earth science that studies the ocean. There are several branches of Marine Science:

Marine Biology or Biological Oceanography, studies the plants, animals and microbes of the oceans and their interaction with their surrounding.

Marine Physics or Physical Oceanography, studies the ocean's physcial parameters such as its temperature, waves, tides and currents.

Marine Chemistry or Chemical Oceanography, studies the chemistry of the ocean and its chemical interaction with the atmosphere.

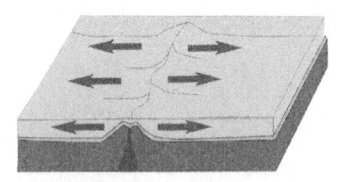

Marine Geology or Geological Oceanography, studies the geology of the ocean floor including plate tectonics.

Paleoceanography studies the oceans as they were in the past, from a few hundred years to billions of years ago.

MARINE SCIENCE

Jacques-Yves Cousteau (1910-1997)

Cousteau

Cousteau, a french oceanographer, along with naval officer Philippe Tailliez and diver Frédéric Dumas, became known as the "mousquemers" ("musketeers of the sea").

In 1950, the great adventure that lasted four decades began when he embarked on the ship Calypso, a former minesweeper transformed into an oceanographic vessel and equipped with diving and scientific research instruments.

He is the world's most famous sea explorer.

🕐 How it all started

The first maritime explorers were the **Phoenicians** and the **Greeks**.

Aristotle (384-322 BC) was a keen observer who was fascinated by zoology and sea creatures.

He distinguished over 500 animal species, classifying them in his book **"History of Animals"** on a scale of perfection, with man at the top.

Aristotle

DAY 1

MARINE SCIENCE

Test your knowledge

Read the following sentences and write T for true and F for false.

Marine science is the science that studies rocks. _____

Aristotle was one of the earliest marine biologists. _____

Marine chemistry is a branch of marine science. _____

Oceanographer studies the oceans. _____

Marine science studies the fisheries. _____

Marine science is a branch of Earth science. _____

Unscramble the words below and write the answers in the boxes on the left.

Csteauou	
graOceanophy	
otBa	

MARINE SCIENCE

 Test your knowledge

Name five branches of marine science.

- _____

- _____

- _____

- _____

- _____

Read the sentences below and fill in the blanks with the appropriate words.

Marine science is also known as _____ and _____.

_____ was a french oceanographer who made underwater documentaries.

_____ _____ is a branch of marine science.

DAY 2

THE OCEAN

> The oceans are responsible for all life, including our own. They contain 97 percent of Earth's water.

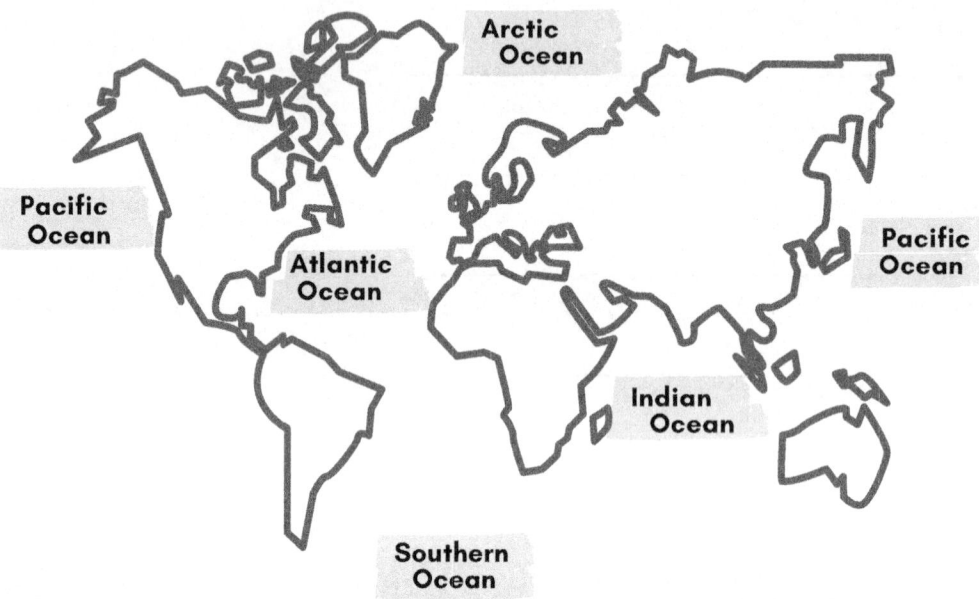

The ocean is a huge interconnected body of water that **moves** through all ocean basins and continents.
There are 5 interconnected ocean basins named:
Atlantic, Pacific, Indian, Arctic and Southern Ocean.
The oceans cover about **70%** of the Earth's surface.

What is the ocean basin?

The ocean basin is the land surface beneath an ocean. Its size and shape vary according to plate tectonic activity, weathering and erosion. The ocean floor has mountains, plains, volcanoes, canyons and other features.

THE OCEAN

How important is the ocean?

The oceans play an important role in **regulating the climate**, **absorbing large amounts of carbon dioxide**, providing most of our **oxygen** and **feeding** a large portion of the human population.

- **50%** of the Earth's oxygen comes from the oceans.
- **97%** of the water on Earth is salt water and is found in the ocean. **Salinity** and **temperature** are two properties of the ocean. They vary throughout the ocean.

The ocean is home to a wide variety of both life and species. It has more diverse species than land.
It is home to the tiniest organisms and to the largest animals on Earth.

Discovering the depths of the ocean is challenging, difficult and expensive. Over 80% of our oceans are not mapped, observed or explored.

Sound Navigation and Ranging, or **sonar**, is a tool for exploring and mapping the ocean. Sound waves travel farther under water than radar and light waves.

DAY 2

THE OCEAN

 Test your knowledge

Use your favourite website to fill in the blanks below using the following words:
Mauna Kea; Mariano Trench; Pacific Ocean

The highest mountain on Earth is in the Ocean.
It is located in the Pacific Ocean and is called _____ ___ .

The lowest point on Earth is in the _____ _____ and is called _____ _____.

Read the sentences below and write T for true, and F for false.

There is a great diversity of organisms in the ocean.   _____

There is a single ocean that covers most of the Earth's surface.   _____

The water in the ocean moves from one place to another.   _____

The ocean floor has many features similar to those of the land.   _____

THE OCEAN

 Test your knowledge

Human activities sometimes have negative impact on the oceans. However, we can keep it healthy and clean. Name three human activities that harm the ocean.

- _____
- _____
- _____

Name three reasons why oceans are vital.

- _____
- _____
- _____

Name two important gases that are regulated by the oceans.

- _____
- _____

DAY 3

WAVES

Waves are created by a generating force like the wind, they cause changes in the water level at the surface, causing the water to rise and fall. Waves are **energy** that moves across the surface of the water.

How are waves formed?

Waves can be caused by earthquakes, volcano eruptions and landslides but the most common ones are surface waves caused by winds.

Wind blowing across the ocean creates friction between air and water molecules, which creates frictional resistance that can be seen as waves on the ocean surface.

The stronger the wind, the bigger the waves.

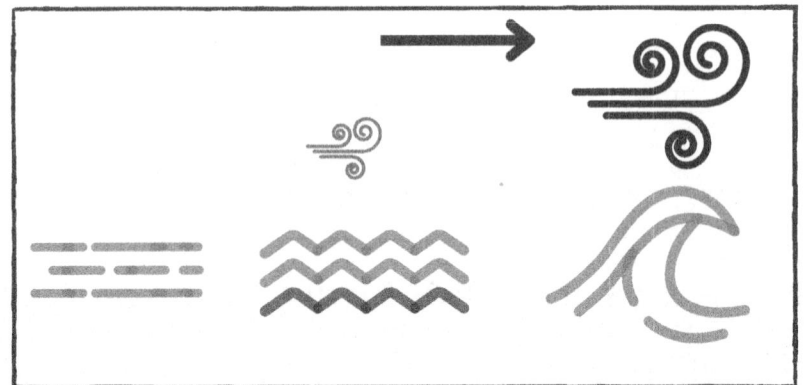

Many other factors influence the size of the waves:
- the depth of the seabed
- the period during which the wind blows
- the amount of water exposed to the wind with no obstruction

WAVES

Parts of a wave

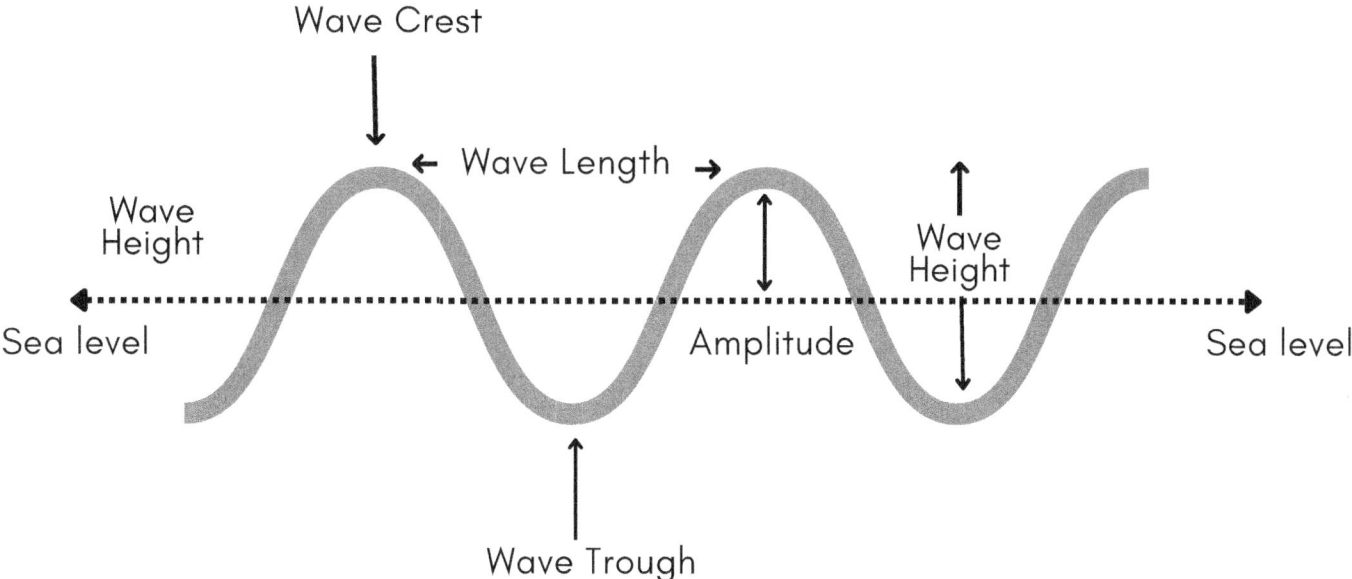

The **crest** of the wave is its highest point. The **trough** of a wave is its lowest point. The distance between two crests or troughs is called the **wavelength**. The **amplitude** is the distance between the trough and the sea level.

Rogue Waves: The biggest waves are called rogue waves, and are capable of drowning boats.
Rogue waves can be higher than 30 meters.
Tsunamis: Tsunamis are a particular kind of waves. They are mostly caused by an earthquake.
When two tectonic plates move, a gigantic amount of energy is liberated leading to a high amount of water displaced and generates enormous waves of 10 to 20 meters.
Tsunamis can also be caused by meteorites crashing into the ocean.

WAVES

 Test your knowledge

Complete the sentences below with the appropriate words.

The stronger the wind, ___ _____ the waves.

Waves are _____ that moves across the surface of the water.

There are different types of waves, the ocean swell is one of them. Ask an adult to help you look at your favourite website to find 5 properties of ocean swell.

_____
_____
_____
_____
_____

Name the 4 factors that influence the size of the waves.

_____
_____
_____
_____

WAVES

 Test your knowledge

Use what you have learned in 10 Days of Geology to draw a diagram showing how the movement of tectonic plates can trigger a tsunami.

Annotate the missing parts of a wave shown in the diagram below.

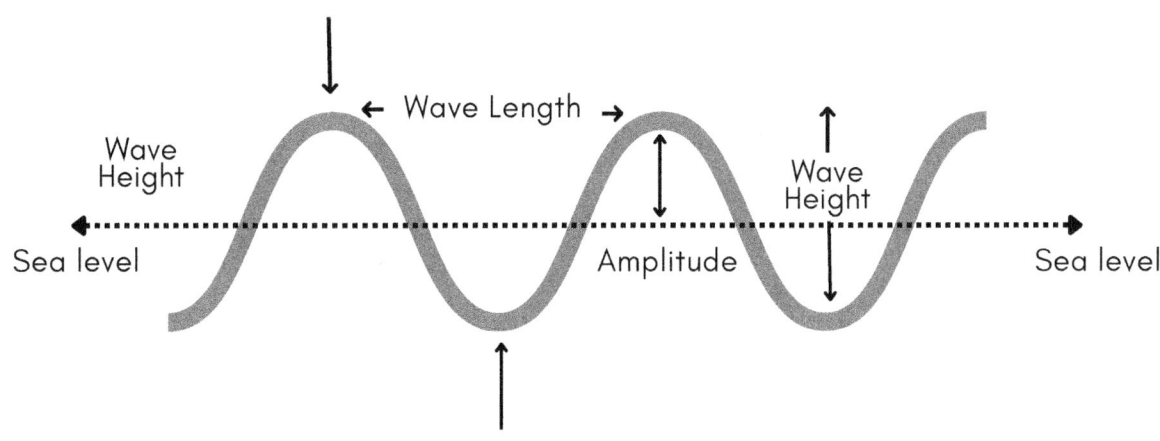

DAY 4 — TIDES

> The tide is a regularly recurring movement of water in the oceans and seas. It results in a rise and fall of the sea level at the same place.

How are tides formed?

Tides are the result of two forces: gravity* and centrifugal force (linked to the rotation of the Earth on itself).

The moon and the sun attract the surface waters of the entire Earth.

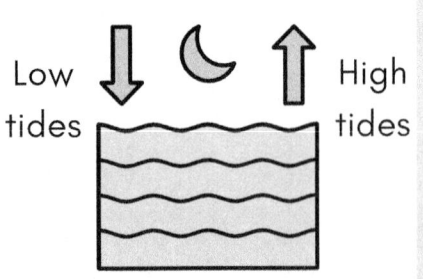

It can be an upward movement, known as a **high tide**, or a downward movement, known as a **low tide**.
The difference in height between the high tide and the low tide is called the **tidal range**.

How it all started...

Isaac Newton (1643 - 1727), an english scientist, discovered the phenomenon of the gravitational attraction of stars to the Earth.

*See definition of gravity in 10 Days Of Space.

16

TIDES

Why are tides different?

Tides vary according to the position of the Moon and the Sun in relation to the Earth's axis, defined by the equator.

Gravitational pull of the Sun and the moon

New Moon   Low tides   **Full Moon**

Low tides

High tides   High tides

Sun

Gravitational pull of the moon

Because the sun is so far away from the Earth, its effect on the tides is half as great as that of the moon.

Most of the tidal movement is therefore due to the Moon.

TIDES

 Test your knowledge

Read the sentences below and fill in the blanks with appropriate words.

Tides are the result of two forces:
_____ and _____ force.

The _____ and the ____ attract the surface waters of the entire Earth.

A _____ tide is when the sea level reaches its highest level.

A ____ tide is when the sea level reaches its lowest level.

The difference in height between the high tide and the low tide is called the _____ range.

Read the sentences below and write T for true, and F for False.

Tides vary according to the position of the Moon. _____

Tides can occur in big lakes. _____

Tides happen regularly. _____

Isaac Newton was the first scientist to explain the tides. _____

TIDES

 Test your knowledge

The amplitude of the water movement varies according to the position of the stars in relation to the Earth's axis. The more they are aligned with the Earth, the greater the amplitude of the tide.

When are the highest tides in the year?

Hint: Look on your favorite website for the definition of equinox.

_____

_____

Annotate the diagram below.

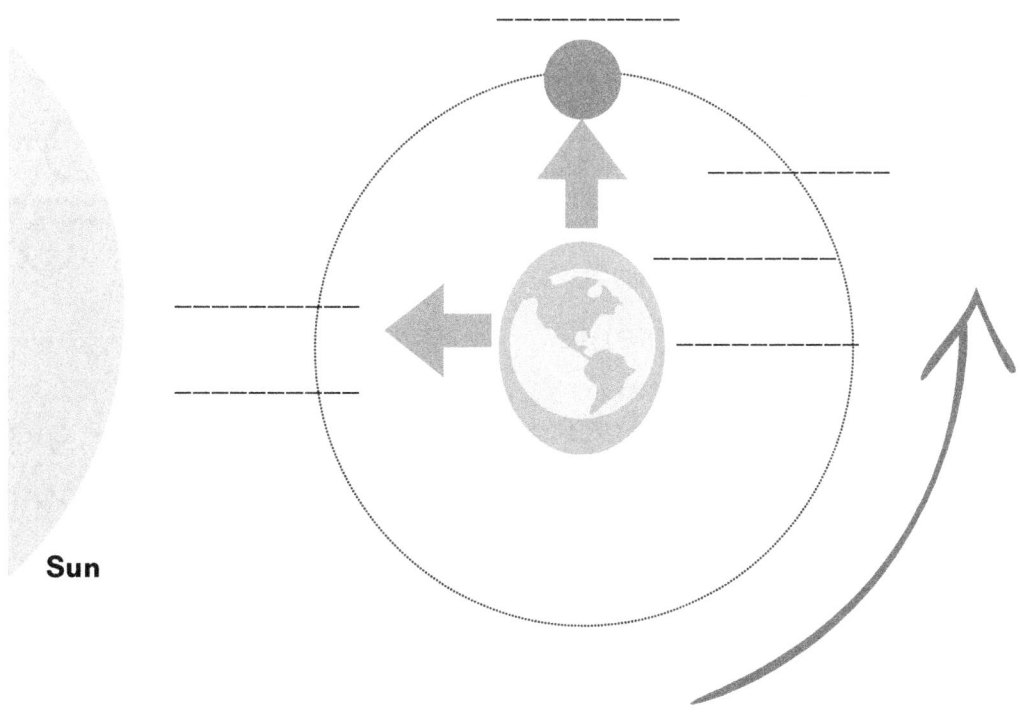

Sun

DAY 5

CURRENTS

The waters of the seas and oceans are constantly moving around the world. All these movements constitute what is known as ocean circulation and are manifested in ocean currents.

These waters move both at the surface and at depth.
These movements are conditioned by several factors:

Thermohaline circulation

* Salinity is the concentration of dissolved inorganic salts in sea water.

The **temperature** and **salinity** of the water varies in different parts of the ocean, resulting in a difference in the density of the water that creates the thermohaline circulation.

Wind

Blowing wind produces currents at the surface of the ocean.

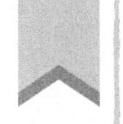

Tides

Tides create the tidal current.

Currents play an important role in regulating global climate, but it also affects local weather conditions and marine ecosystems by transporting larva and nutrients over long distances.

CURRENTS

**There are two main types of currents
Surface currents and the Deep currents**

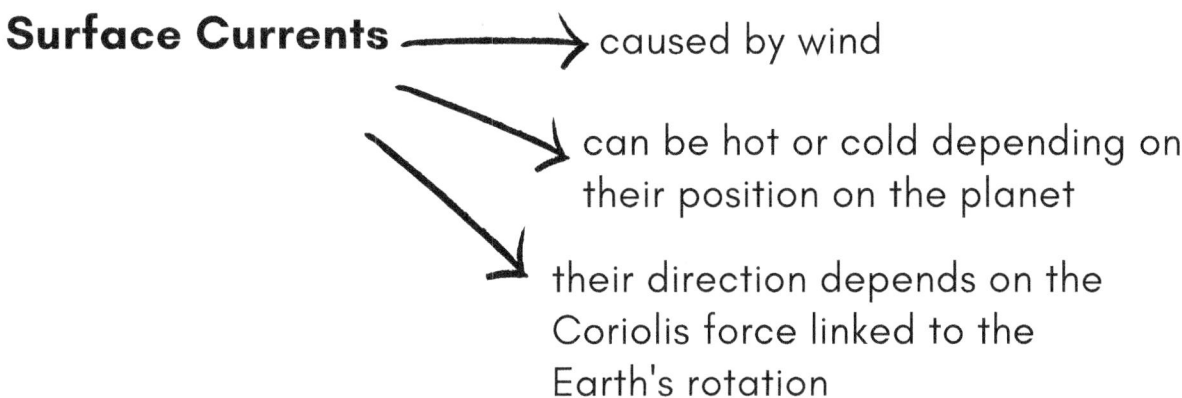

Surface Currents → caused by wind

↘ can be hot or cold depending on their position on the planet

↘ their direction depends on the Coriolis force linked to the Earth's rotation

Ocean surface currents in both hemispheres move in rather circular paths called **gyres**.

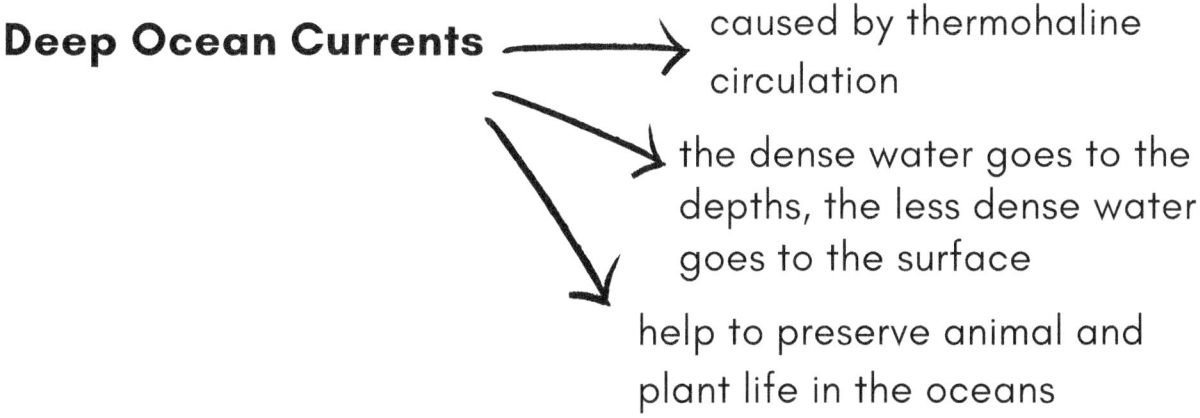

Deep Ocean Currents → caused by thermohaline circulation

↘ the dense water goes to the depths, the less dense water goes to the surface

↘ help to preserve animal and plant life in the oceans

The main ocean currents

Gulf Stream; Labrador Current; North Equatorial Current; South Equatorial Current; North Equatorial Counter Current; South; Equatorial Counter Current; Kuroshio Current; Alaska Current; California Current.

CURRENTS

 Test your knowledge

_____ **Currents** ⟶ caused by _____

can be ___ or ____ depending on their position on the planet

their direction depends on the Coriolis _____ linked to the Earth's _____

Ocean surface currents in both hemispheres move in rather circular paths called _____.

____ _____ **Currents** ⟶ caused by _____ circulation

the _____ water goes to the _____, the less _____ water goes to the _____

help to preserve _____ and _____ life in the oceans

Give the name of three main ocean currents:

_____

_____

_____

CURRENTS

 Test your knowledge

EL NIÑO

El Niño (Spanish for 'the kid') is a warm current in the South Pacific Ocean that occurs between Australia, Indonesia and South America. It has a very important effect on climate and weather patterns.

Watch a documentary about El niño.
Make a list of 5 interesting facts you learned from the documentary.
Ask an adult to help you choose a website that you can use for your research.

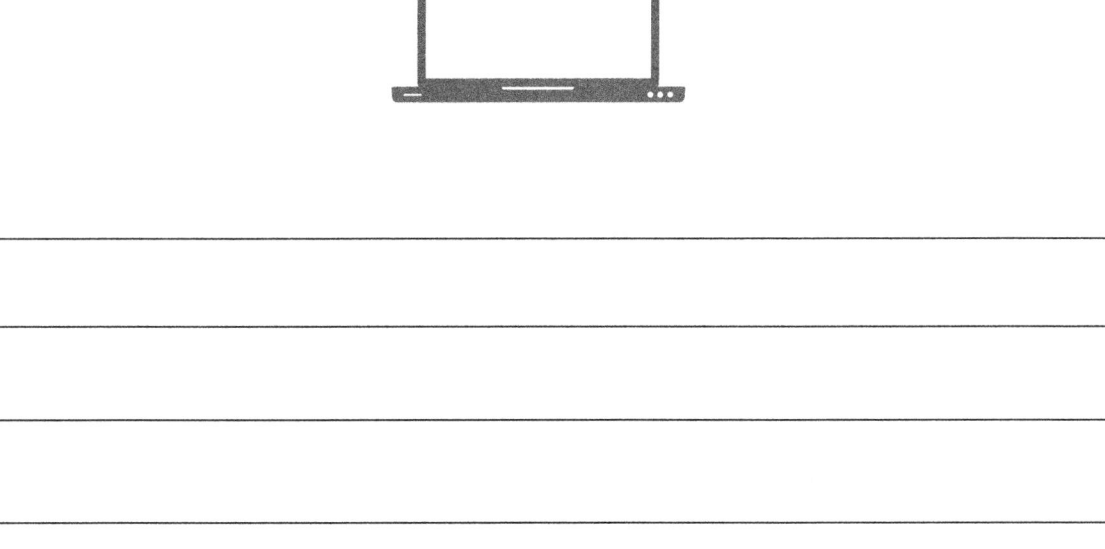

_____
_____
_____
_____
_____

DAY 6

OCEAN LIFE

The oceans are home to a rich and diverse life, including plants and small animals such as corals and anemones.

What are corals?

Corals are small animals with a calcareous skeleton. These animals accumulate on the sea floor, forming coral reefs.

The Great Coral Reef is located in Australia. More than 1,500 species of fish live in this 2,300 km long coral reef, which is also a haven for a wide variety of aquatic plants

Australia

Similar to corals, **sea anemones** are found on the sea floor. These animals have a base attached to a hard surface and a ring of tentacles surrounding the mouth.

Sea Anemones

24

OCEAN LIFE

Sea anemones are the habitat of the clown fish, like the one in the animated film! Finding N _ _ _ (Can you guess the name of that film?)
The fish feeds the anemone by exchanging nutrients, while the plant protects the fish from predators with its tentacles.

 **Phytoplankton** are very tiny algae. They are essential for feeding the fish. They also consume carbon dioxide to form oxygen like all plants.

Mangroves are trees that rest on the water but whose tops remain on the surface. Often located near the sea and oceans, mangroves can survive in salt water.

OCEAN LIFE

 Test your knowledge

The outer Great Barrier Reef is home to many species of fish. Use your favorite website to find the names of the fish that live there and write down their colors.

1- _____

2- _____

3- _____

4- _____

5- _____

6- _____

7- _____

8- _____

Read the sentences below and fill in the blanks with the appropriate words.

_____ are trees that rest on the water but whose tops remain on the surface.

_____ are very tiny algae. They are essential for feeding the fish. They also consume carbon dioxide to form oxygen like all plants.

OCEAN LIFE

In the box below, draw and label a coral reef. Include animals such as seahorses, clownfish, and sea turtles that live on coral reefs.

Use your favourite website to find the locations of coral reefs and write them below. What do they all have in common?

_____

_____

_____

JELLYFISH

Jellyfish are gelatinous marine animals mostly living in sea water. They are able to sting with their tentacles.

What are jellyfish made of?

A jellyfish's body is 95% water. The body of a jellyfish is rather soft, shaped like an umbrella that closes, pushing water to one side and propelling the jellyfish to the other.

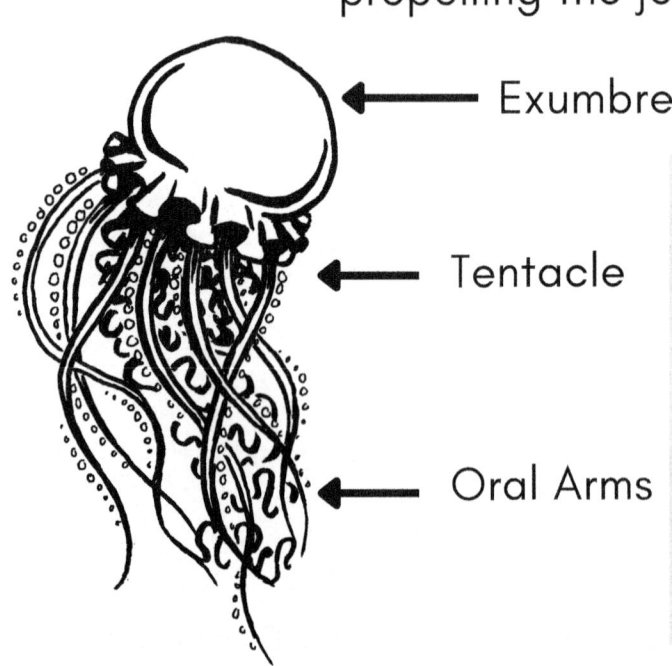

← Exumbrella shape bell

← Tentacle

← Oral Arms

Tentacles composed of stinging cells, called **cnidocytes.**
These are miniature spear guns, each connected to a venom reservoir. Each jellyfish has thousands of them.

These cells come into contact with the skin of swimmers or fish, they inject their venom through a tiny harpoon, causing itching. This is their technique for capturing their prey: they catch them with their tentacles and paralyse them with their venom before eating them.

JELLYFISH

The jellyfish is an animal that floats, that swims but that cannot resist the sea currents therefore jellyfish are part of the plankton.

A group of jellyfish is called a **smack**.

The jellyfish has no brain, heart, lungs or gills. It breathes through its body wall. It has a digestive system with a mouth between the tentacles, a stomach, muscles and nerves.

Where are they found?

Jellyfish are found everywhere in the world.
They like warm water and the increase in ocean temperature favours their growth and extends their reproduction period.
Jellyfish proliferate because of fertiliser pollution which encourages the reproduction of the plankton that constitute their food, and from overfishing, which eliminates their predators.

The jellyfish *Turritopsis nutricula* has the particularity of being able to reverse the ageing process. It can rejuvenate its cells and go from being a jellyfish to a polyp.

DAY 7

JELLYFISH

 Test your knowledge

Read the sentences below and fill in the blanks with the appropriate words.

Jellyfish are _____ marine animals mostly living in sea water. They are able to sting with their _____.

The jellyfish is an animal that _____, that swims but that cannot resist the sea _____ therefore jellyfish are part of the _____.

Ask an adult to help you search your favorite website for answers to the following questions.

What is the biggest jellyfish?
What is the tiniest jellyfish?
What is the deadliest jellyfish?

_____

_____

_____

JELLYFISH

 Test your knowledge

Jellyfish can survive in low oxygen environments and warm waters, unlike other species. Climate change and human activities are increasing water temperatures and releasing nutrients into the water.

 → This release of nutrients increase the growth of phytoplankton.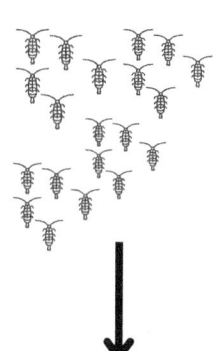

This causes the jellyfish population to increase and to expand in many different areas thtoughout the world. ← When phytoplankton die, oxygen levels drop, killing fish but not jellyfish.

How do we, as individuals, contribute to the proliferation of jellyfish?

_____

_____

DAY 8
SHARKS

Did you know that?

Sharks are fishes from the *elasmobranch* family.

They don't have any bones, their skeleton is cartilaginous.

Sharks are older than dinosaurs: they have been present in the oceans for more than 400 million years.

Like all fish, sharks filter oxygen from the water with their gills.

Sharks can develop and use over 20,000 teeth in their lifetime.

The shark families

The **hammerhead shark** has a hammer-shaped head. It has electrical sensors in its head. It uses these to find its prey, even if they are hiding.

The **great white shark** can find a drop of blood in 25 gallons of water. It can weigh up to 2000 kg and measure up to 5 metres. It has up to 300 teeth with five rows of teeth at any given time.

Leopard sharks are easily recognisable due to the dark spots on their back, like leopards.

SHARKS

Sharks are dangerous to humans. They confuse humans with their natural prey such as seals. However, attacks are very rare and sharks are not the most deadly animals.

Number of fatal attacks per year

 **Sharks: 9**    **Lions: 250**

 **Snakes: 100,000**    **Cows: 20**

How does a shark move?

The shark's fin on its back is used as a rudder. The shark turns left and right by leaning it.
The tail moves from side to side and allows the shark to move forward.
The lateral fins are used by the shark to maintain its balance.

SHARKS

 Test your knowledge

Fill in the blanks with appropriate words.

The _____ _____ has a head shaped like a hammer. It has _____ sensors in its head. It uses it to find _____ , even if they are hiding.

The _____ _____ _____ can find a drop of blood in 25 gallons of water. It has ____ teeth.

Every year, around _ humans are killed by sharks. Sharks are not the deadliest animals and shark attacks are very ____ . Every year, lions kill ___ humans and cows __ .

During most shark attacks on humans, they confuse humans with their _____ _____ like _____ .

Sharks are older than _____ : they are in oceans for more than ___ _____ years.

Like all the _____ , sharks filter _____ from water with their _____ .

SHARKS

 Test your knowledge

Help the shark move through the water! Complete the following diagram.

When the shark wants to move left and right: it uses its ___ . Circle it on the shark below.

When the shark wants to move forward: it uses its ____. Circle it on the shark below.

The shark wants to maintain equilibrium: it uses its _____. Circle it on the shark below.

DAY 9

AQUACULTURE

> Aquaculture is the cultivation of aquatic organisms and plants.

 **How it all started . . .**

Humans started farming in water 4000 years BC. Egyptians and chinese were growing fishes and plants.

Why do we do aquaculture?

Aquaculture helps meet the growing demand for seafood, provides healthy protein for people in developing countries and reduces pressure on wild fish.

How is it done?

Aquaculture can be carried out in natural environments.

Aquaculture can be practised on land, using onshore **tanks**.

Floating cages are used to raise fish in sea water, ponds and rivers.

36

AQUACULTURE

Aquaculture is an environmentally friendly activity.
50% of the seafood consumed by humans comes from aquaculture. It prevents the fishing of fish at sea.
It can help save endangered species and is more efficient than farming.
For every Megacalorie used to feed the animal, you get:

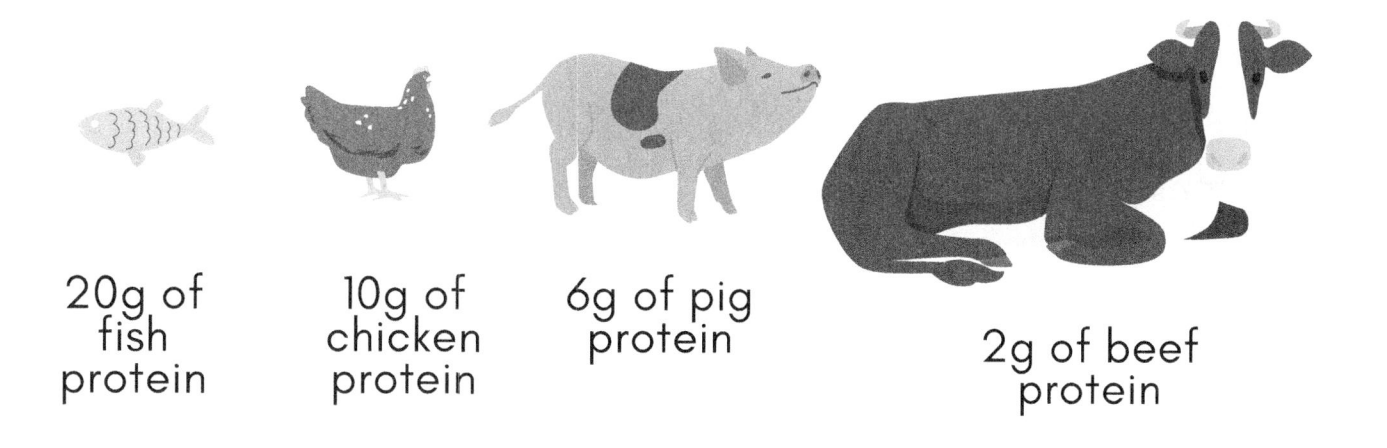

20g of fish protein

10g of chicken protein

6g of pig protein

2g of beef protein

However, there are some disadvantages:

Fish escape from farmed ponds, contaminating wild fish with lice and other diseases.

Aquaculture requires a high consumption of drugs to treat the fish, which pollutes the water.

🚩 The largest aquaculture production in the world is in China.
The United States is in sixth place, just behind the European Union.

DAY 9

AQUACULTURE

Test your knowledge

Ask an adult to help you search your favourite website for a documentary on aquaculture. Watch it and answer the question below.
What do farmed fish eat?

_____

For 1 Megacaloire of food given to an animal how much grams of protein can we obtain?

Fish:

Chicken:

Pig:

Beef:

List three advantages of aquaculture.

- _____

- _____

- _____

List two disadvantages of aquaculture.

- _____

- _____

AQUACULTURE

Test your knowledge

Ask an adult to help you search your favourite website for a documentary on sustainable aquaculture.
Draw a diagram of fish farming and a diagram of algal production in the box below.

DAY 10

OCEAN POLLUTION

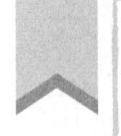

Ocean pollution is caused by human activities. Waste is produced by humans and dumped in landfills. Some of this waste is washed away and ends up in the oceans.

There are two main sources of pollution in oceans:

TRASH: Waste is dumped in landfills or is not managed properly.

It is then carried away by the winds and accumulates in rivers and oceans. Among them, plastic is a major source of ocean pollution.

CHEMICALS: human activities release a lot of chemicals in the environment and in water. Some of them will contribute to the proliferation of algae, which could be dangerous.

Plastic, a new continent

Plastic is accumulating in the oceans. The amount of plastic in the oceans is so high that, thanks to ocean currents, a new solid "island" of accumulated plastic has appeared in the Pacific Ocean.

OCEAN POLLUTION

Plastic Accumulation

The plastic is thrown in the bin.

Plastic is landfilled but washed away by rain and wind.

Plastic is ingested by marine animals. It is also cut into pieces to form dangerous microplastics.

Algae Bloom

The release of chemicals such as nitrogen or phosphorus, for example from fertilisers, promotes the growth of algae. Some algae can release toxins that are very harmful to animals, humans and the environment. These harmful algal blooms are micro-organisms that deplete fish stocks, destroy fish farms and can carry diseases and even cause death to humans and large marine animals.

DAY 10

OCEAN POLLUTION

Test your knowledge

Illustrate the process of ocean pollution.

OCEAN POLLUTION

Test your knowledge

Unscramble the words below and write the answers in the boxes to the left.

ollutonip	
lgeaa	
sictlpa	
ntriunte	
thsar	
mcehilasc	
filtiezers	
mrcoisaticlps	
oolbm	
lfliinadl	

What new words have you learned?

Please feel free to evaluate and leave a review.

We'd love to hear from you so we can create quality content for you.

Follow our author page for updates on new releases and improved recommendations.

Thank you!

Printed in Great Britain
by Amazon